¡FiESTA!
PUBLICATIONS

W9-ABU-957

LA HORA
TIME

This book provides bilingual materials to teach a fun and comprehensive unit on TIME. Included is a teacher's instruction section with details for each project along with ideas to use throughout the classroom. Discover TIME using skills in reading, math, and spelling. Both Spanish and English versions of each project are included in one book!

Cover Photos:

Photo www.comstock.com

© 1995 PhotoDisc Incorporated

© Photodisc

ISBN 1-59441-400-9

Dear Family Letter (pages 8–9)

Dear Family,

We are starting a unit about time. We will learn about reading clocks, telling time, and many other things relating to time.

Please join us by including time games, lessons, or discussions at home. Family discussions will help reinforce the concepts we are learning in class!

Sincerely,

Send this note home with students to let families know what is happening in the classroom. The letter introduces families to the upcoming unit about time.

Time Certificate (pages 10–11)

This is a great way to recognize and reward students as they progress through the TIME unit.

Use the Time Certificates as a specific incentive when students finish a defined list of projects or as a general award when the unit is complete. The certificates make a great classroom bulletin board display and provide students with take-home diplomas that they can be proud of.

Copy the certificates onto colorful paper or let students color their own certificates as a classroom art project.

Time Cards (pages 12–35)

The time cards included in this book can be used in a variety of creative ways to make learning with flash cards fun and interesting.

FLASH CARDS
Make different flash card decks of varying degrees of difficulty to use as assessment tools. Display transparencies of the cards for reference during classroom discussions.

ASSEMBLY INSTRUCTIONS

Copy the desired time cards onto colorful paper or card stock and cut out. Copy the English cards on one side and copy the Spanish cards on the other side. Or, copy the word cards on one side and the analog clock or digital numerals on the other. Laminate cards for permanent use in the classroom or make sets for each student to use at home.

CONCENTRATION
(using clock face cards, Spanish word cards, English word cards, and digital time cards)

This ever-popular game helps students develop memory and matching skills. Concentration works best when played in small groups.

There are several variations of "Time Concentration." Younger students can match clock faces to the same clock faces. Increase difficulty by mixing and matching combinations. For example, students can match cards with analog clock faces to cards with the same digital times, etc.

ASSEMBLY INSTRUCTIONS

Copy the desired time cards onto construction paper or card stock and cut out. Laminate cards for permanent use.

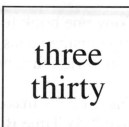

HOW TO PLAY
1. Mix up cards and place them facedown in rows.
2. Have students take turns choosing two cards at a time. If a student chooses two cards that match, he takes another turn. If there is no match, he turns the cards facedown and the next player takes a turn. The player with the most matched pairs wins the game!

My Time Book (pages 36–39)

Students can create and color their own books about time.

These make great story-starter books. Write a variety of time story starters on the inside pages before making copies. For example, write "At 7:30, I" on one of the pages. Then, have students read the story starter and draw clock hands to match the time listed. Finally, have them write paragraphs about what they usually do at that time or have them write fictional stories about what they would like to do at that time. Use this opportunity to have a discussion about A.M. and P.M.. Explain to students that A.M. and P.M. can make the difference between day and night. For example, if the clock says 7:30, students can write that they usually finish their homework by this time. Or, they could write that they like to eat breakfast at this time. Have students share their finished books with the class.

ASSEMBLY INSTRUCTIONS

Copy one book for each student. Copy cover pages onto construction paper or card stock and copy inside pages onto 8½" x 11" (21.6 cm x 27.9 cm) white paper. Assemble and bind books using brass fasteners or staples.

These books make a great take-home project. Have students complete several books to create their own "My Time Book" libraries. Finished books also make an excellent bulletin board display.

Bulletin Board Ideas

- Copy a clock or clock face pattern (below and pages 6–7) onto a transparency. Place it on an overhead projector and trace the image onto butcher paper. Use enlarged clocks to decorate bulletin boards or as borders.

- Start the time unit by creating a clock bulletin board. Give each student the large clock face and hands patterns (page 7) to decorate. When students finish decorating the clocks, have them punch holes in the centers of the clocks and in the ends of the clock hands. Have them attach the hands to the clocks with brass fasteners. Then, have each student write a story about her favorite time of day. Post the stories on a bulletin board along with the clocks. Have each student manipulate her clock's hands so that the clock corresponds to the time in her story. Title the display *My Favorite Time of Day*.

- Copy one clock pattern (below) for each activity or subject in the daily class schedule. Program a sentence strip with each activity or subject title and draw the correct time on a clock. Display the clocks and sentence strips on a bulletin board. Remind young students that when the classroom clock matches the time displayed, it is time for the corresponding activity.

- Have students help create this bulletin board while simultaneously assessing their knowledge of the class schedule. Give each student a laminated copy of a clock pattern (below and pages 6–7) and a laminated index card. List the class schedule on a piece of chart paper and display it on a bulletin board. Name an activity from the class schedule. Have students use a write-on/wipe-away marker to draw clock hands that show the time at which that activity occurs. Then, have them write the digital equivalent on the index cards. Choose a clock and an index card with the correct time to post beside that activity. Continue until you have posted a clock and index card for each activity.

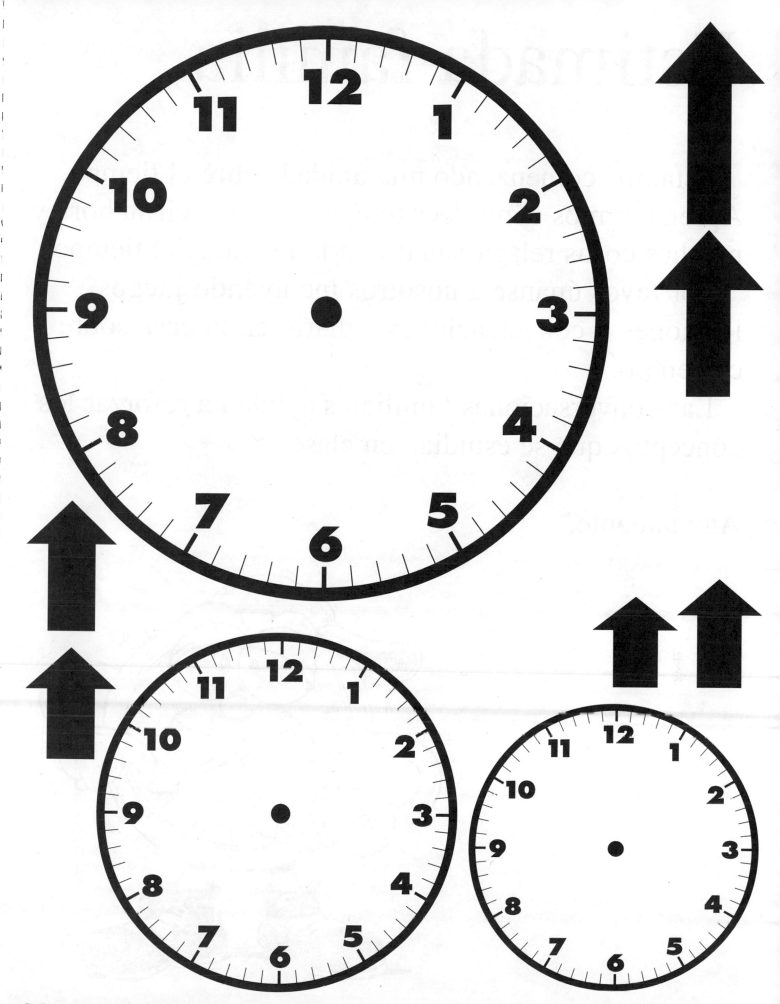

Estimada familia,

Estamos comenzando una unidad sobre el tiempo. Aprenderemos cómo leer relojes, cómo decir la hora y muchas cosas relacionadas con la medida del tiempo.

Por favor únanse a nosotros incluyendo juegos, lecciones o conversaciones a diario en la casa sobre el tiempo.

Las conversaciones familiares ayudan a reforzar los conceptos que se estudian en clase.

Atentamente,

Dear Family,

We are starting a unit about time. We will learn about reading clocks, telling time, and many other things relating to time.

Please join us by including time games, lessons, or discussions at home. Family discussions will help reinforce the concepts we are learning in class!

Sincerely,

LA HORA

CERTIFICADO

¡Yo sé cómo decir la hora!

Nombre: _____

¡Felicidades!
Has aprendido sobre
los relojes y cómo decir
la hora.

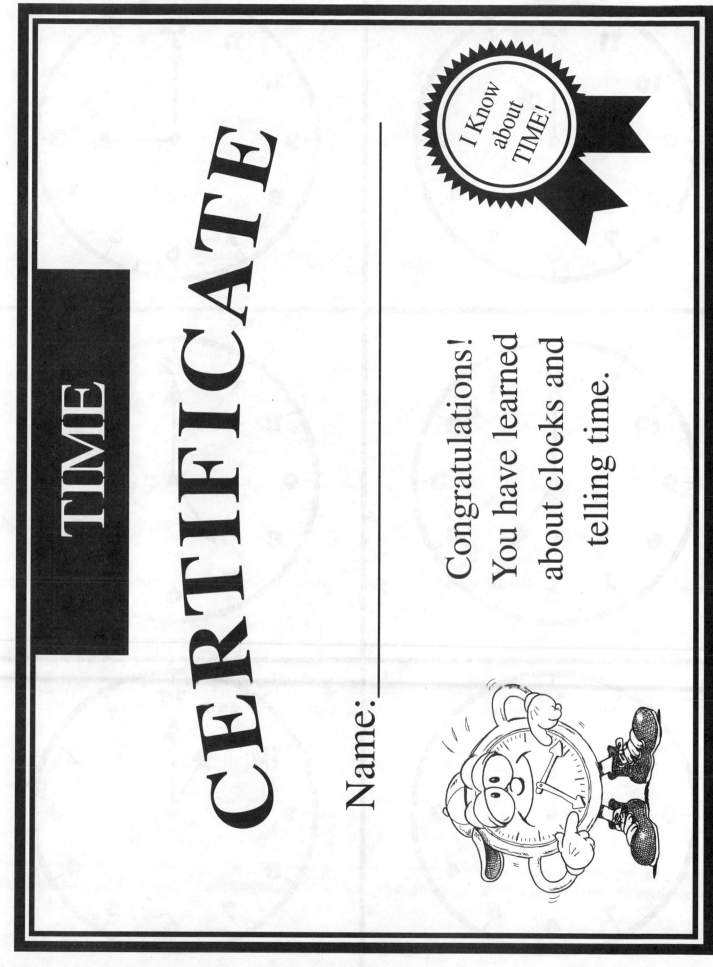

TIME

CERTIFICATE

I Know about TIME!

Name: _____

Congratulations! You have learned about clocks and telling time.

11

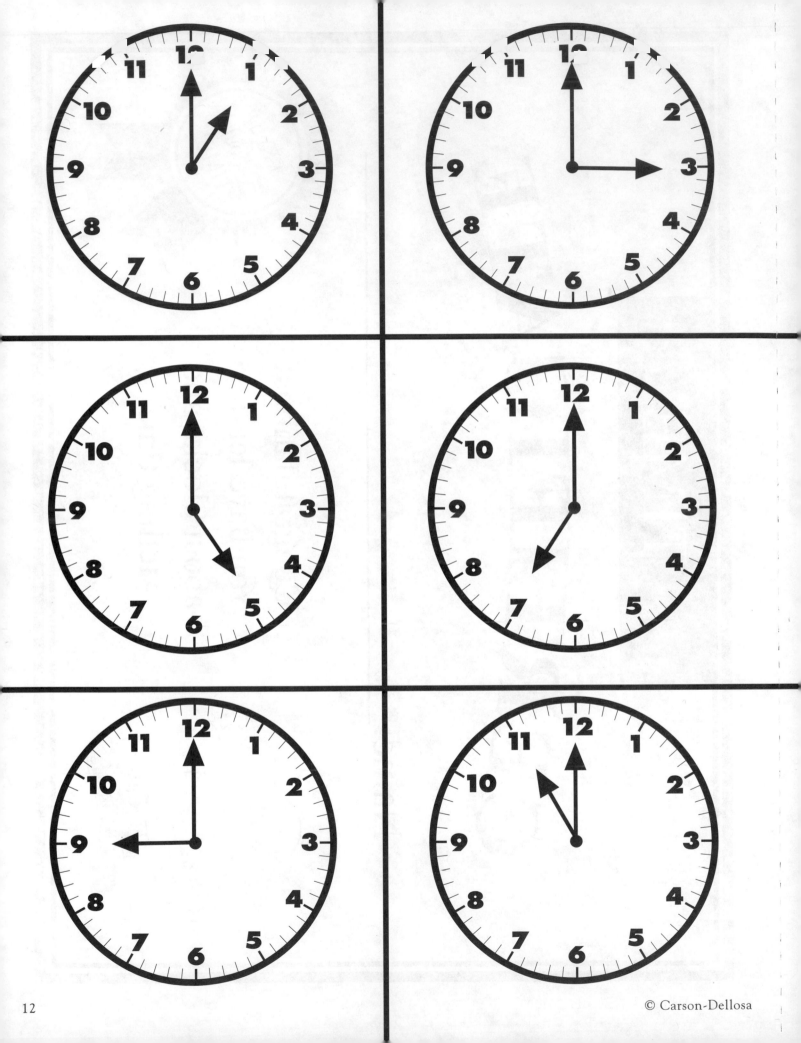

es la una	son las tres
son las cinco	son las siete
son las nueve	son las once

three o'clock	one o'clock
seven o'clock	five o'clock
eleven o'clock	nine o'clock

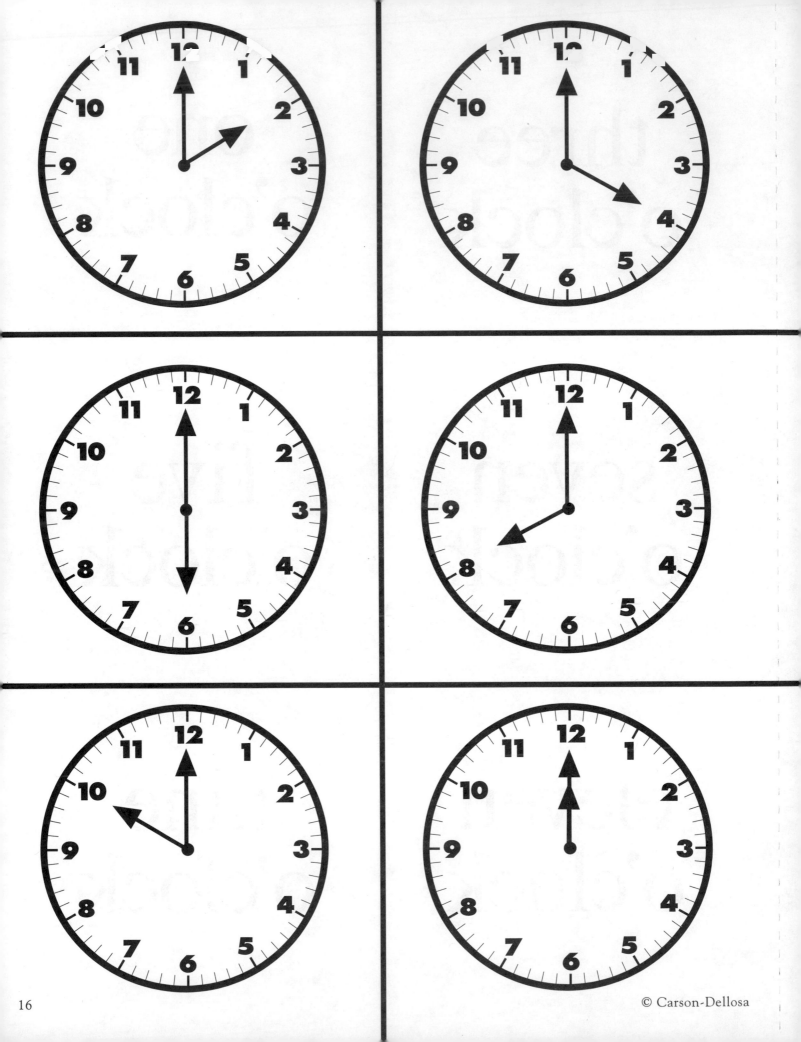

son las dos	son las cuatro
son las seis	son las ocho
son las diez	son las doce

four o'clock	two o'clock
eight o'clock	six o'clock
twelve o'clock	ten o'clock

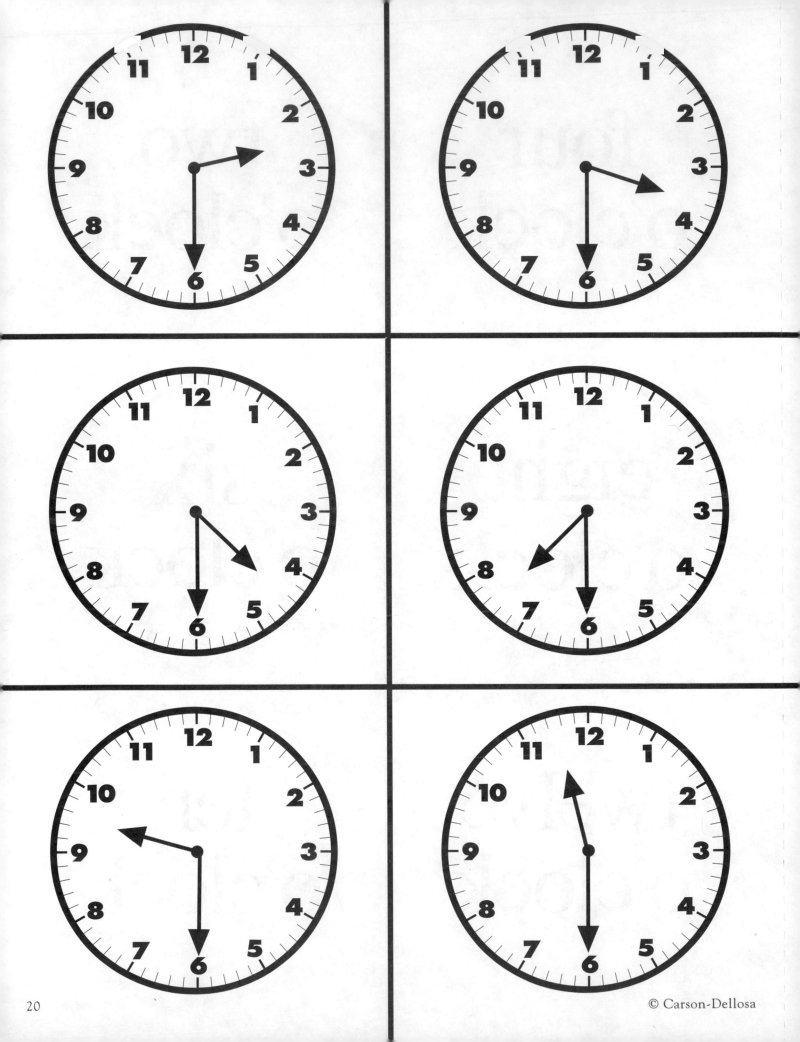

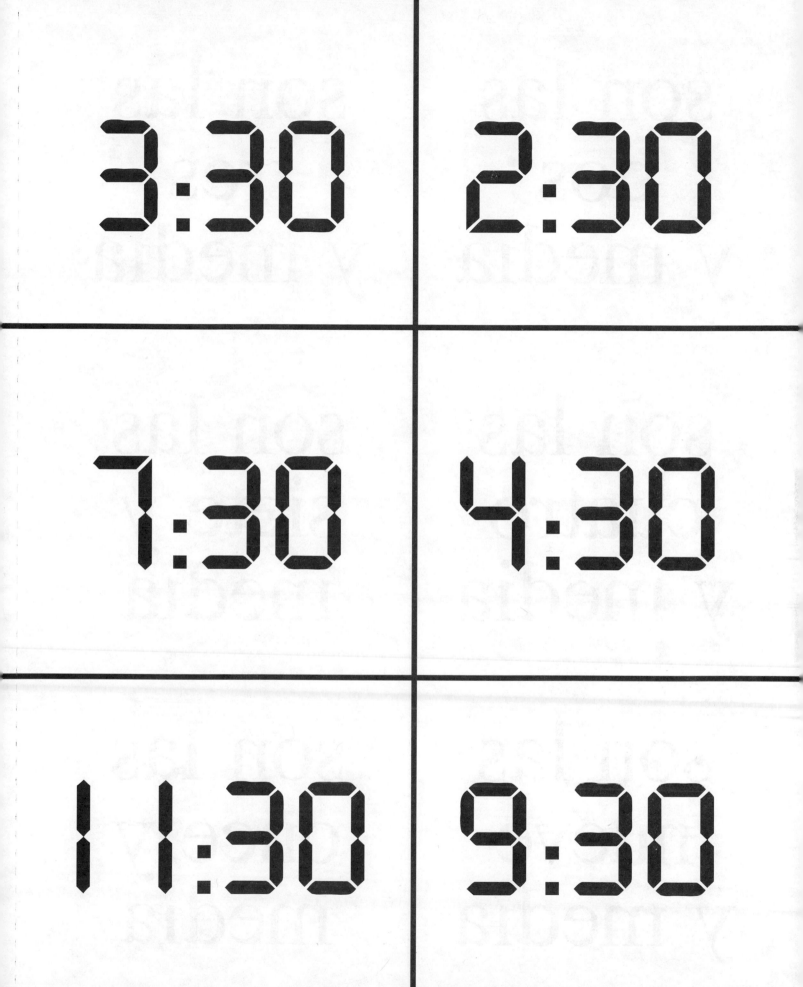

3:30   2:30

7:30   4:30

11:30   9:30

son las dos y media	son las tres y media
son las cuatro y media	son las siete y media
son las nueve y media	son las once y media

three thirty	two thirty
seven thirty	four thirty
eleven thirty	nine thirty

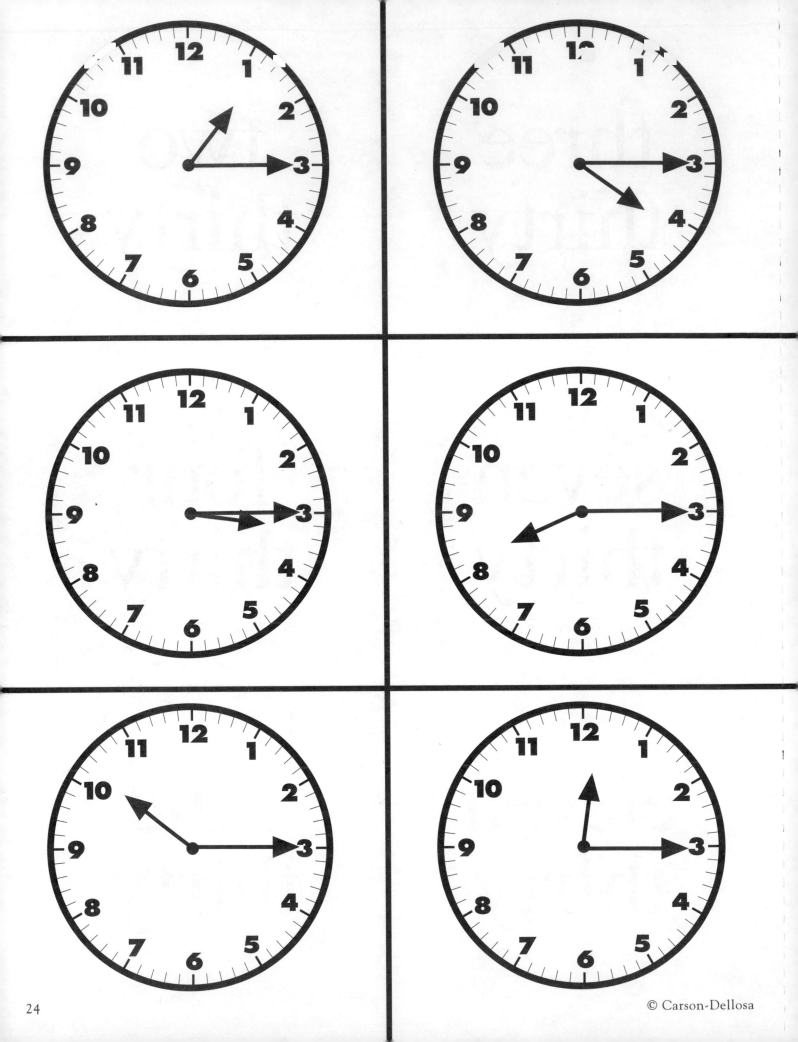

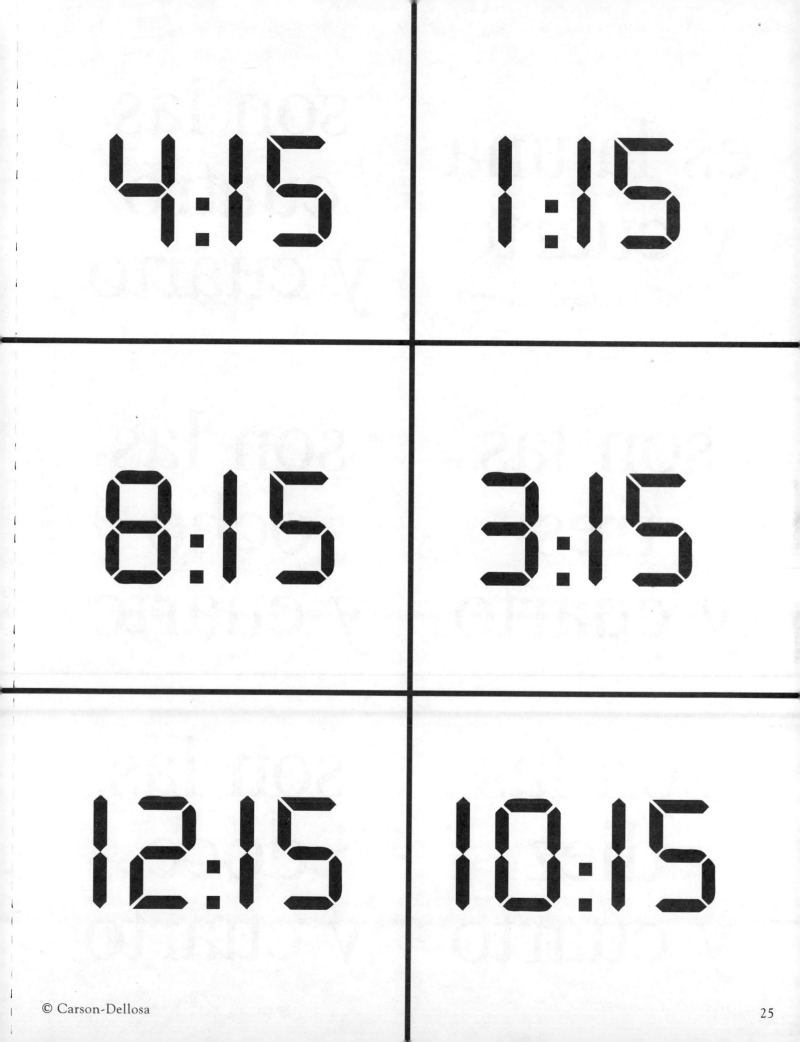

4:15

1:15

8:15

3:15

12:15

10:15

es la una y cuarto	son las cuatro y cuarto
son las tres y cuarto	son las ocho y cuarto
son las diez y cuarto	son las doce y cuarto

four fifteen	one fifteen
eight fifteen	three fifteen
twelve fifteen	ten fifteen

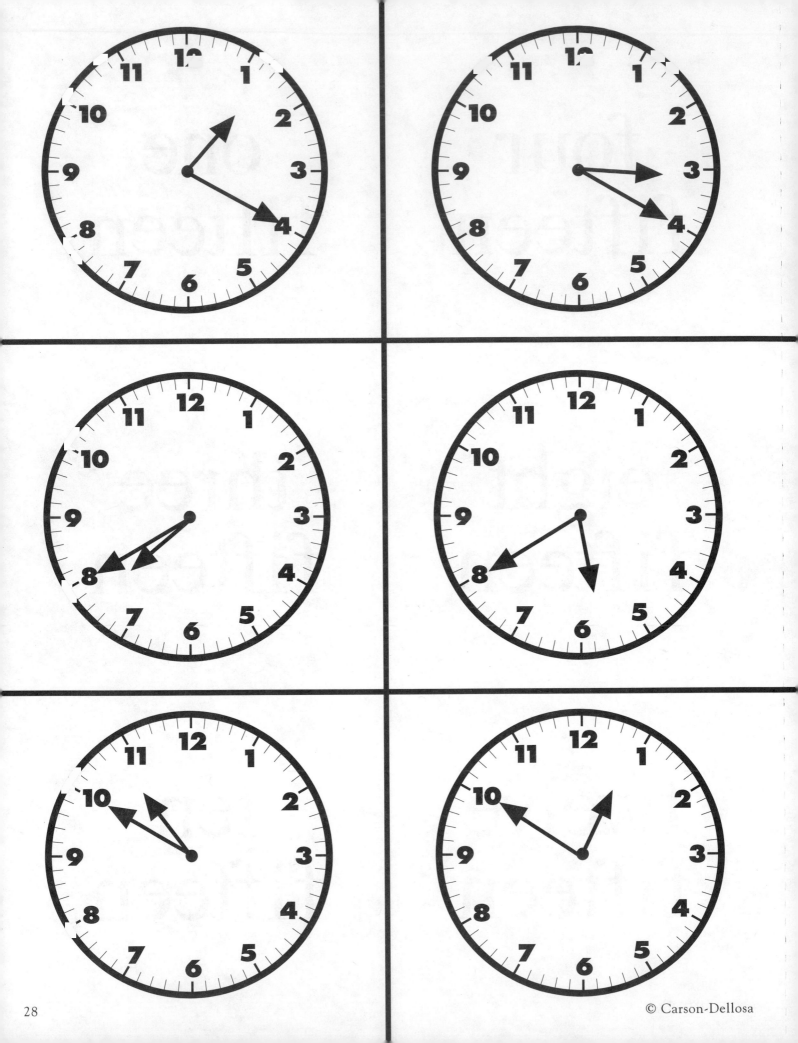

3:20

1:20

5:40

7:40

12:50

10:50

es la una y veinte	son las tres y veinte
son las ocho menos veinte	son las seis menos veinte
son las once menos diez	es la una menos diez

three twenty	one twenty
five forty	seven forty
twelve fifty	ten fifty

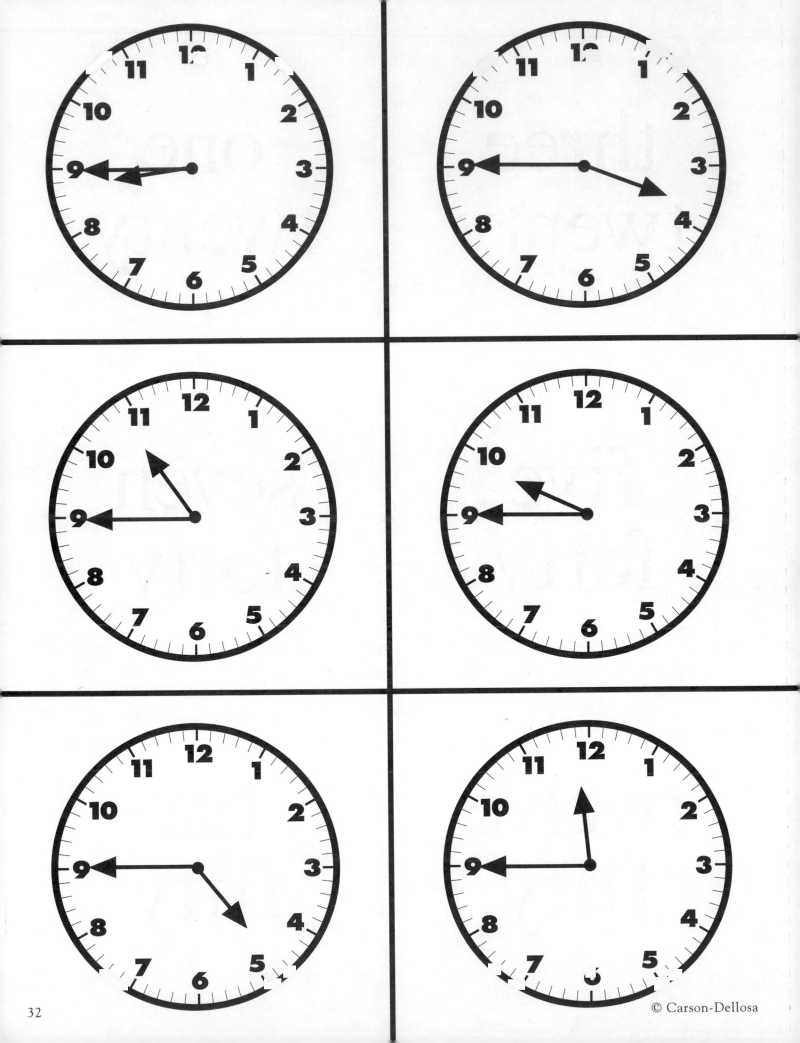

3:45

8:45

9:45

10:45

11:45

4:45

son las nueve menos cuarto	son las cuatro menos cuarto
son las once menos cuarto	son las diez menos cuarto
son las cinco menos cuarto	son las doce menos cuarto

three forty-five	eight forty-five
nine forty-five	ten forty-five
eleven forty-five	four forty-five

Mi libro de
La hora

Nombre: _____

My
Time
BOOK

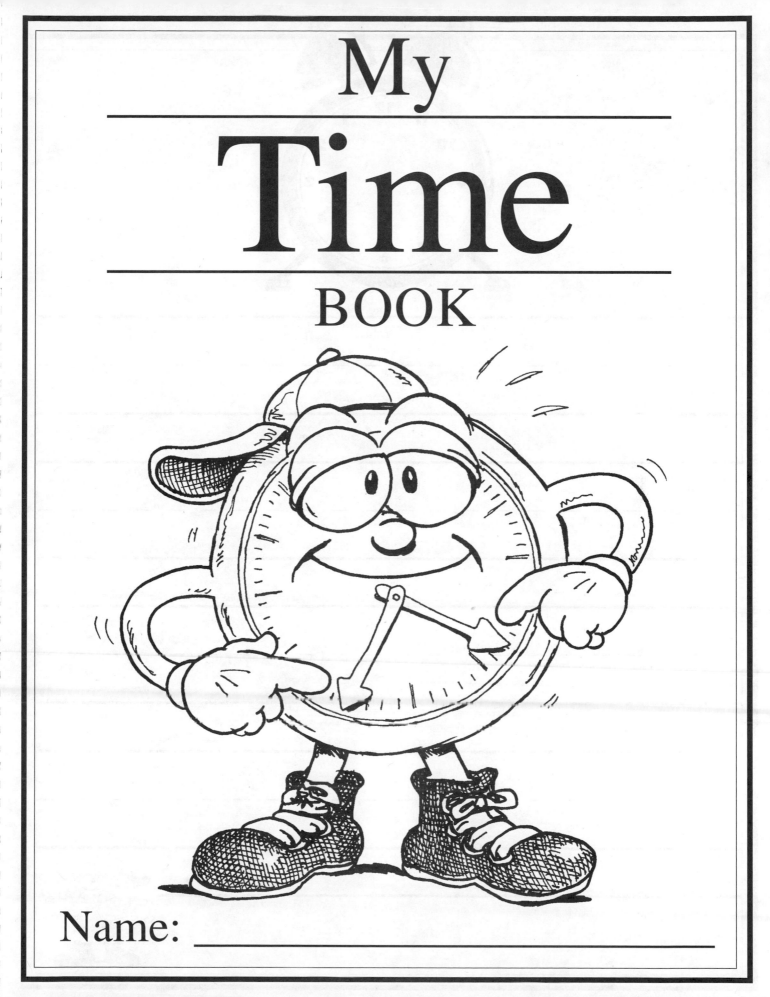

Name: _____

Escoge la hora

Traza una línea desde el
reloj hasta la hora correcta.

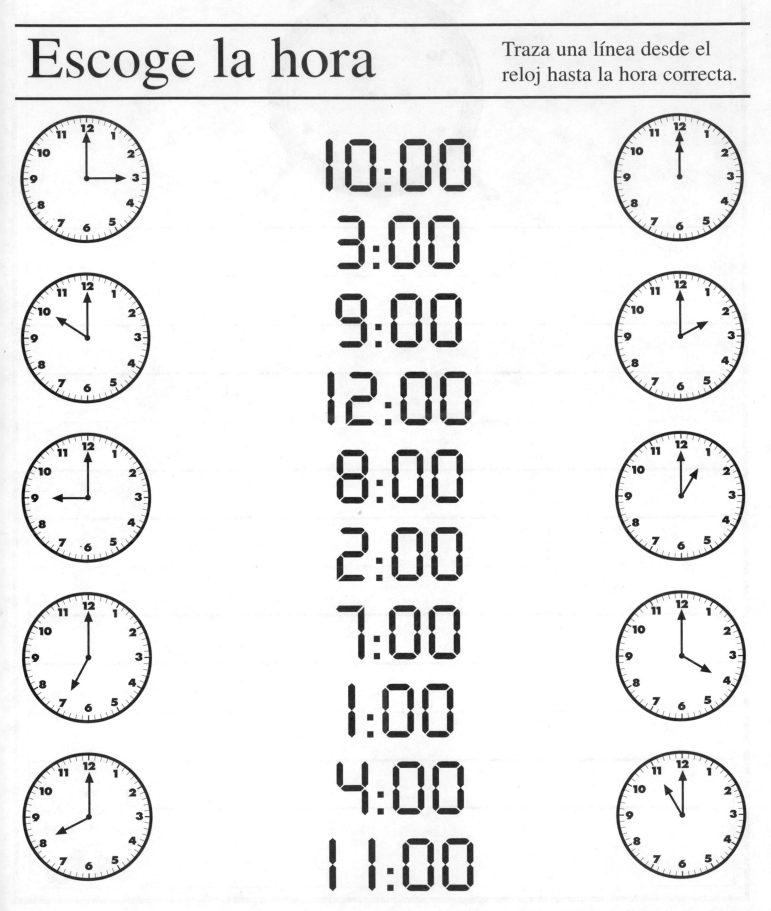

10:00

3:00

9:00

12:00

8:00

2:00

7:00

1:00

4:00

11:00

Name:_____

Time Match

Draw a line from the clock to the correct time.

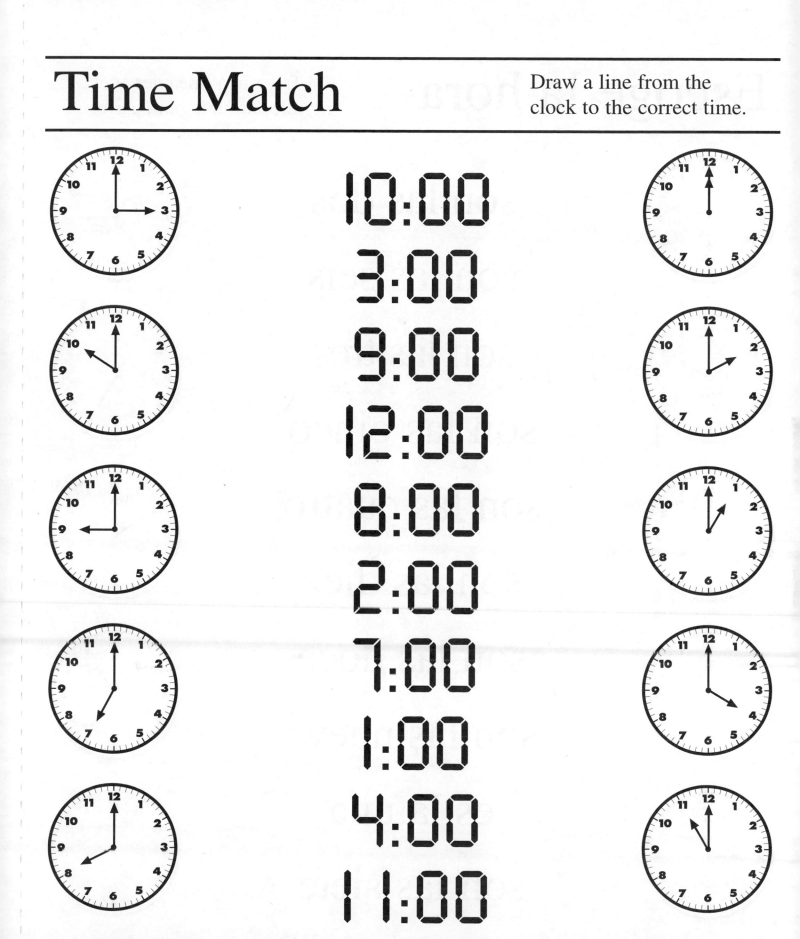

10:00

3:00

9:00

12:00

8:00

2:00

7:00

1:00

4:00

11:00

Escoge la hora

Traza una línea desde el reloj hasta la hora correcta.

son las dos

son las seis

son las tres

son las cinco

son las cuatro

son las diez

son las doce

son las nueve

es la una

son las siete

Time Match

Draw a line from the clock to the correct time.

two o'clock

six o'clock

three o'clock

five o'clock

four o'clock

ten o'clock

twelve o'clock

nine o'clock

one o'clock

seven o'clock

Escoge la hora

Traza una línea desde el
reloj hasta la hora correcta.

son las doce y media

son las siete y media

son las cuatro y media

es la una y media

son las ocho y media

son las dos y media

son las tres y media

son las cinco y media

son las seis y media

son las diez y media

Time Match

Draw a line from the clock to the correct time.

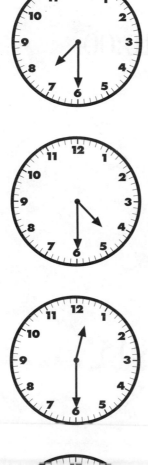

twelve thirty

seven thirty

four thirty

one thirty

eight thirty

two thirty

three thirty

five thirty

six thirty

ten thirty

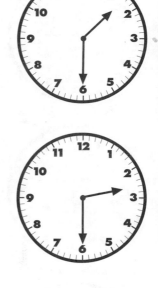

Marca la hora.

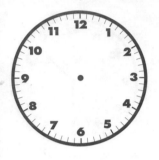 Guillermo salió de la casa a las 10:00.

 José desayunó a las 7:30.

 El maestro va a la escuela a las 8:15.

 La mamá de Tomás va al trabajo a las 10:45.

 Comemos el almuerzo al mediodía.

Draw the time.

 Bill left home at 10:00.

 Joe ate breakfast at 7:30.

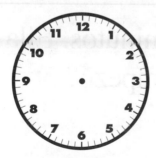 The teacher goes to school at 8:15.

 Tom's mother goes to work at 10:45.

 We eat lunch at noon.

Marca la hora.

 Luis almorzó al mediodía. Tres horas después se comió un bocadillo. ¿A qué hora se comió Luis su bocadillo?

 Juan se fue a la escuela a las 8:00. Era una caminata de 10 minutos. ¿A qué hora llegó?

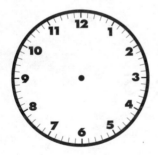 Ana caminó por media hora. Ella empezó a las 7:15. ¿A qué hora terminó?

 Lisa jugó con su gato por veinte minutos. Ella terminó a las 9:30. ¿A qué hora empezó?

 Tomás se acuesta a las 8:30. Él lee por 30 minutos antes de acostarse. ¿A qué hora empieza a leer?

Draw the time.

 Luis ate lunch at noon. Three hours later, he ate a snack. What time did Luis eat his snack?

 Bill left for school at 8:00. It was a 10-minute walk. What time did he get to school?

 Ann walked for half an hour. She started at 7:15. What time did she finish?

 Lisa played with her cat for 20 minutes. She finished at 9:30. What time did she start?

 Tom goes to bed at 8:30. He reads for 30 minutes before bed. What time does he start reading?

Marca y escribe la hora.

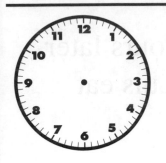 Rita cena a las 6:00. Le toma media hora para terminar. ¿A qué hora termina?

_____

 David jugó con Marcos por dos horas. Terminaron de jugar a las 3:00. ¿A qué hora empezaron? _____

Maria fue a la tienda a las 2:15. Volvió a casa a las 3:00. ¿Cuánto tiempo estuvo fuera de casa? _____

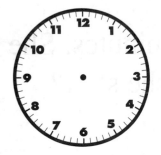 Susana jugó a "bingo" por una hora y quince minutos. Empezó a las 9:00. ¿A qué hora terminó? _____

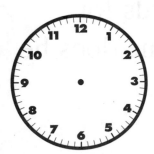 Carlos se va a trabajar a las 7:15. Él trabaja por 8 horas.¿A qué hora vuelve a casa Carlos? _____

Draw and write the time.

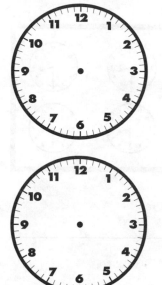

Rita eats dinner at 6:00. It takes her half an hour. What time does she finish? _____

David played with Mark for 2 hours. They finished playing at 3:00. What time did they start? _____

Mary went to the store at 2:15. She came home at 3:00. How long was she gone?

_____

Susan played bingo for 1 hour and 15 minutes. She started at 9:00. What time did she finish? _____

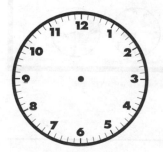

Carlos goes to work at 7:15. He works for 8 hours. What time does Carlos go home?

_____

Cuenta los relojes

Cuenta la cantidad de relojes.
Escribe el número en letras.

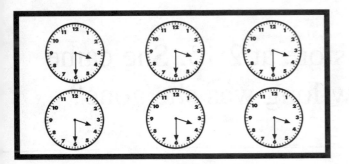

(Ejemplo)

tres

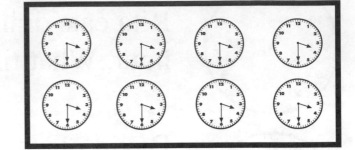

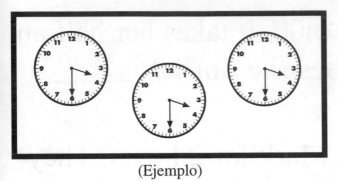

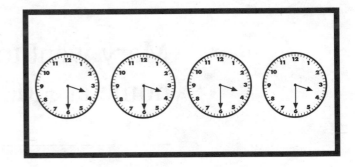

Count the Clocks

How many clocks are there?
Write the number word.

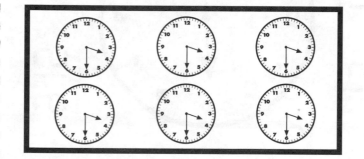

(Example)

three

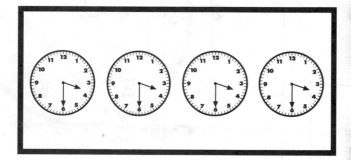

Nombre: _____

¿Qué hora es?

Haz un círculo alrededor de la hora correcta.

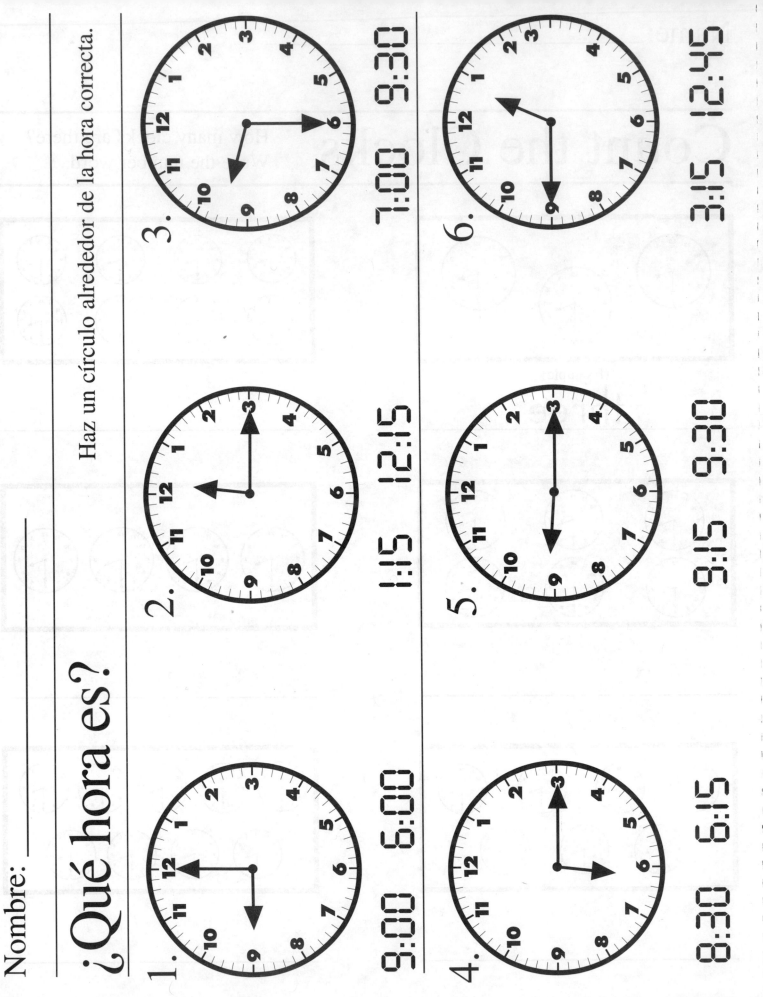

1.   9:00   6:00

2.   12:15   1:15

3.   7:00   9:30

4.   8:30   6:15

5.   9:15   9:30

6.   3:15   12:45

Name: _____

What Time Is It?

Circle the correct time.

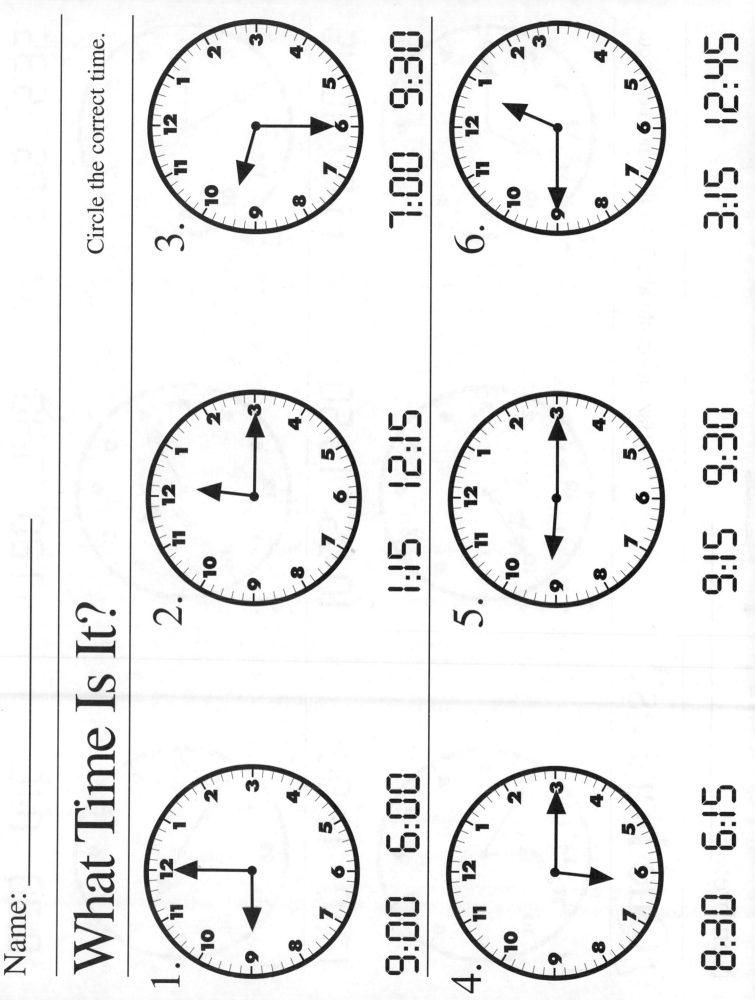

1. 9:00 6:00 9:09

2. 1:15 1:15 12:15

3. 7:00 9:30 9:6

4. 8:30 8:30 6:15

5. 9:15 9:30 9:8

6. 3:15 12:21 12:47

Nombre: _____

¿Qué hora es?

Haz un círculo alrededor de la hora correcta.

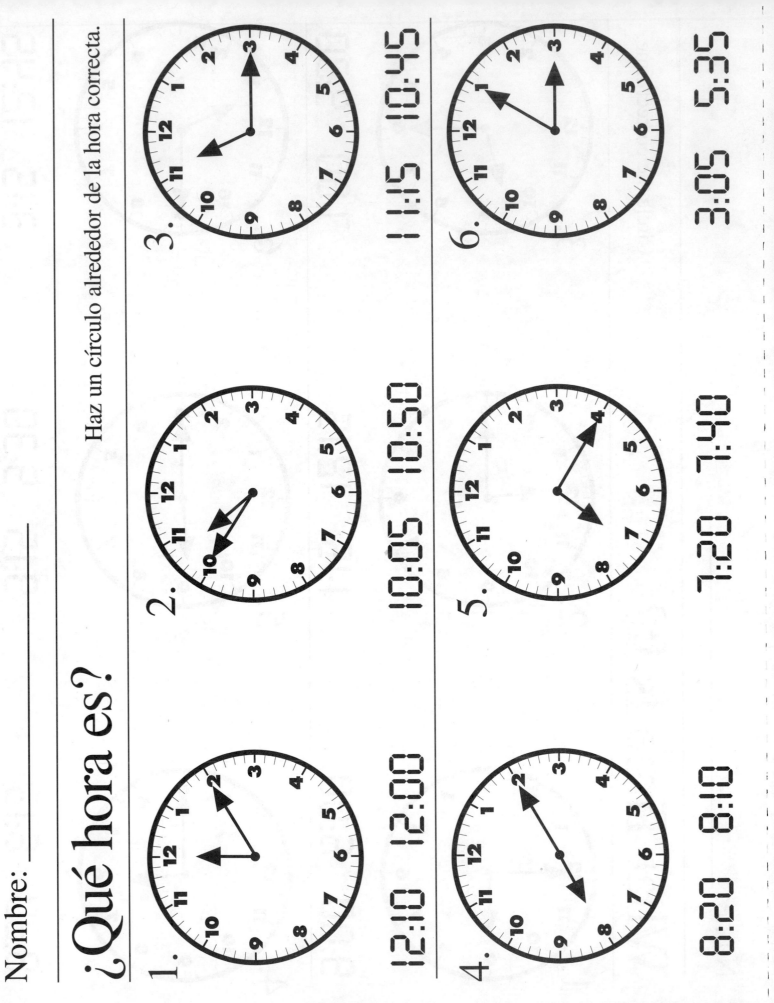

1. 12:10 12:2 12:00

2. 10:05 10:01 10:50

3. 11:15 10:45

4. 8:20 8:8 8:10

5. 7:20 1:20 1:40

6. 3:05 5:5 5:35

Name: _____

What Time Is It?

Circle the correct time.

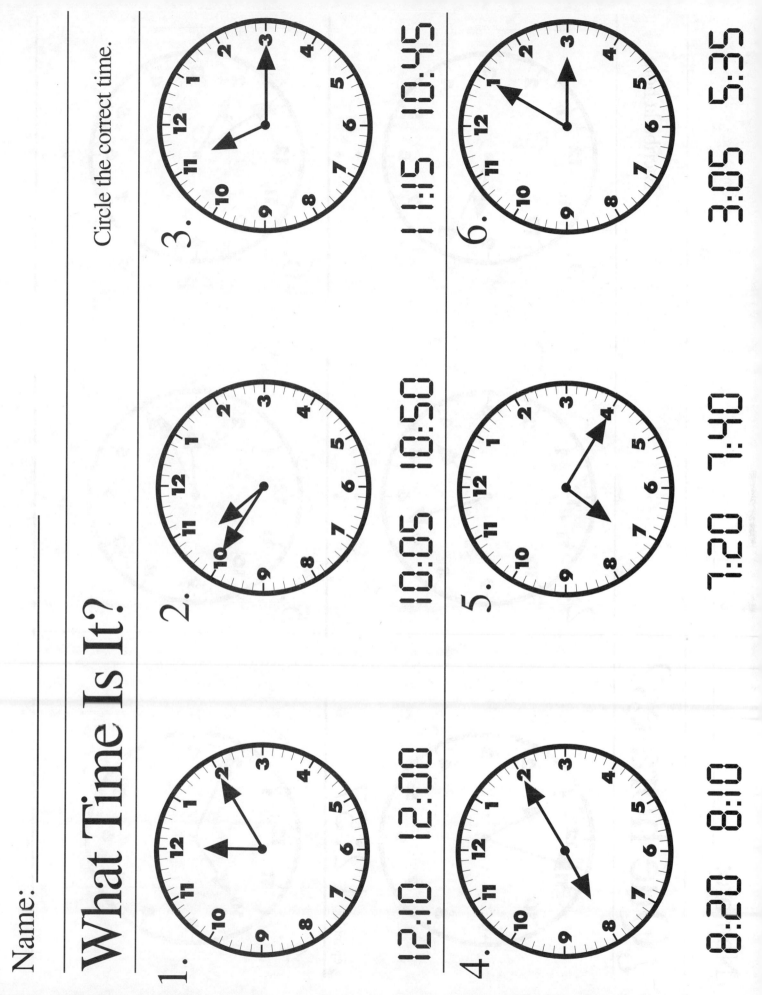

1.   12:10   12:2

2.   10:05   10:0

3.   11:15   10:45

4.   8:20   8:10

5.   1:20   7:40

6.   3:05   5:35

Nombre: _____

¿Qué hora es?

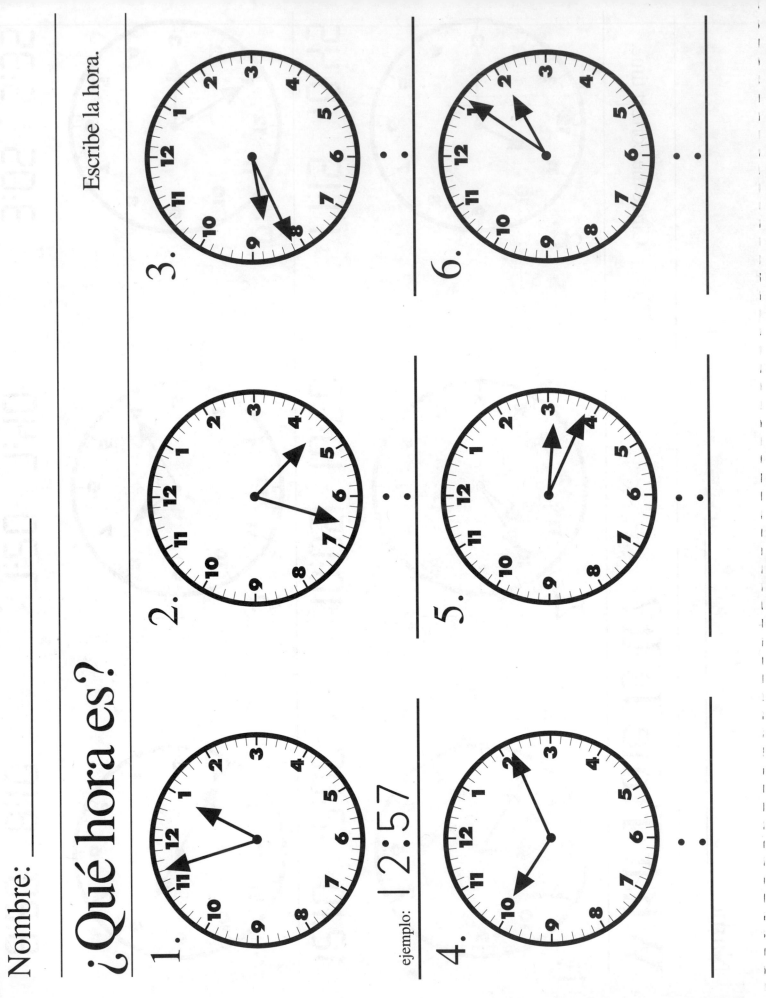

1.

2.

3.

ejemplo: | 2:57

4.

5.

6.

Name: _____

What Time Is It?

Write the time.

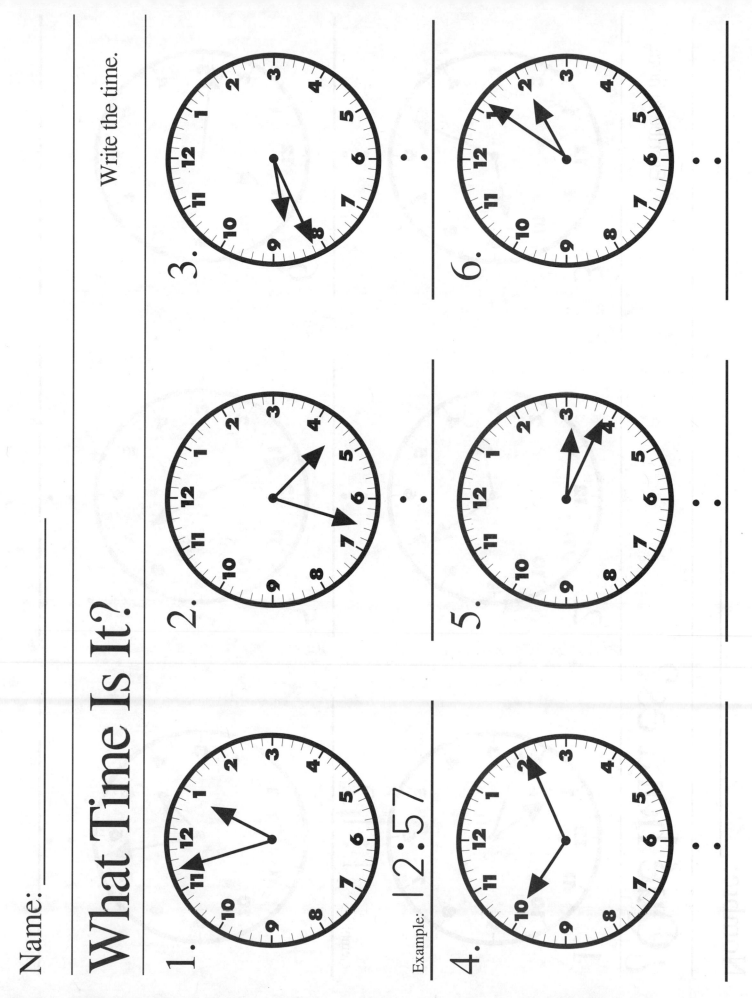

1. _____

2. _____

3. _____

Example: 12:57

4. _____

5. _____

6. _____

Nombre: _____

¿Qué hora es?

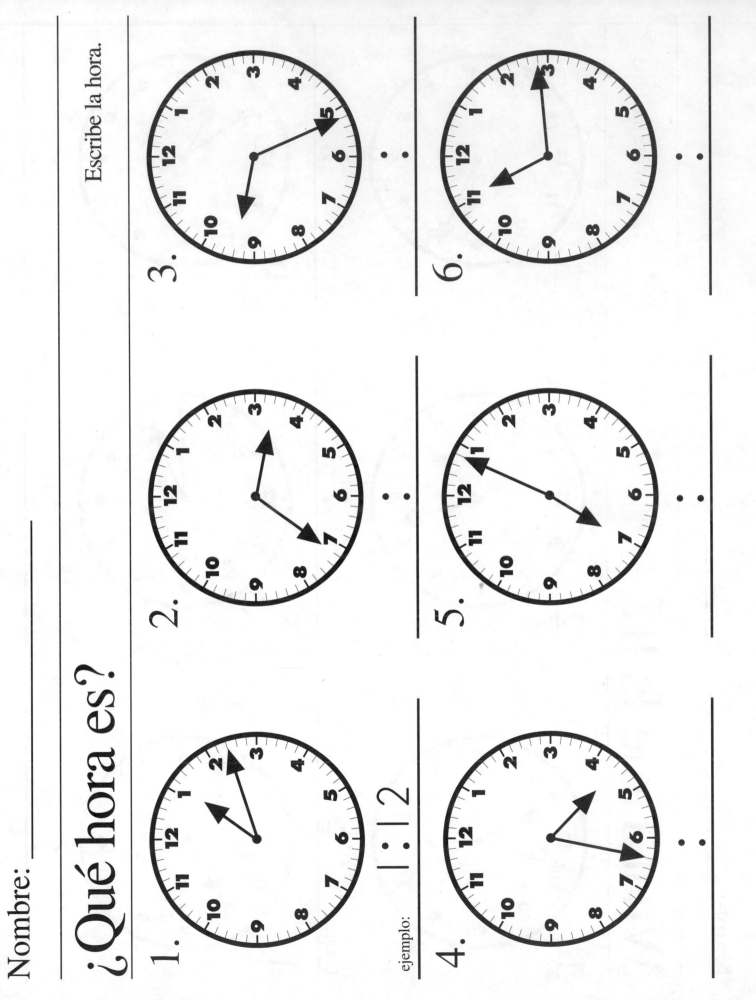

1.

2.

3. · ·

ejemplo: 1:12

4. · ·

5. · ·

6. · ·

Name: _____

What Time Is It?

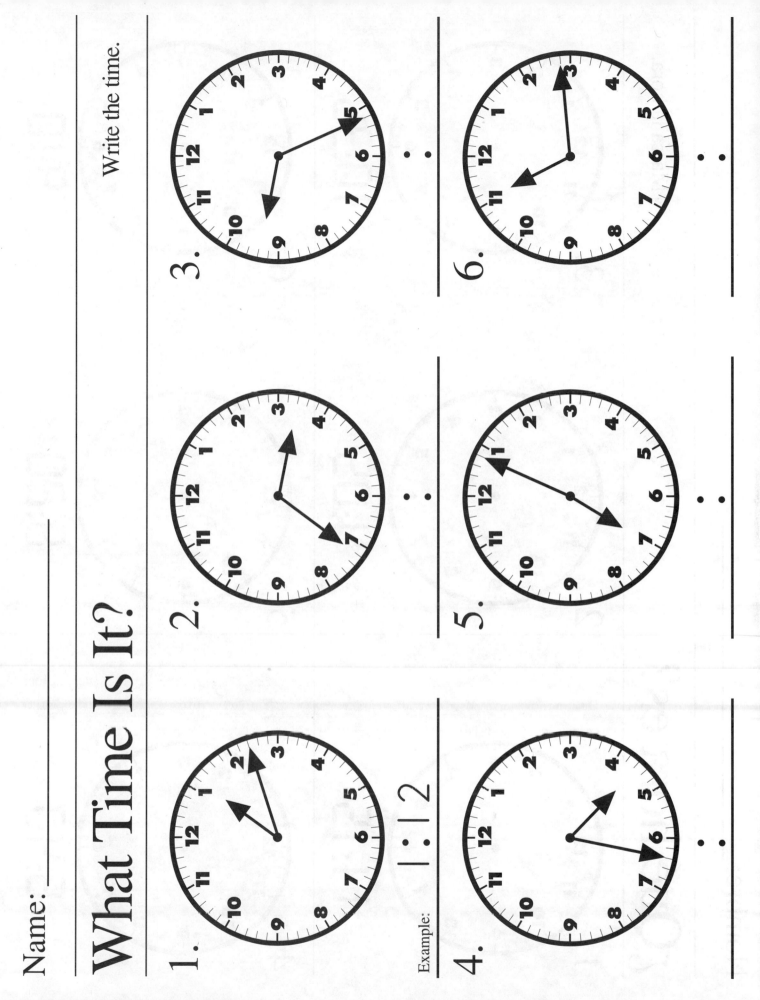

1. ____

Example: |:|2

2. ____

3. ____

4. ____

5. ____

6. ____

Nombre: _____

¿Qué hora es?

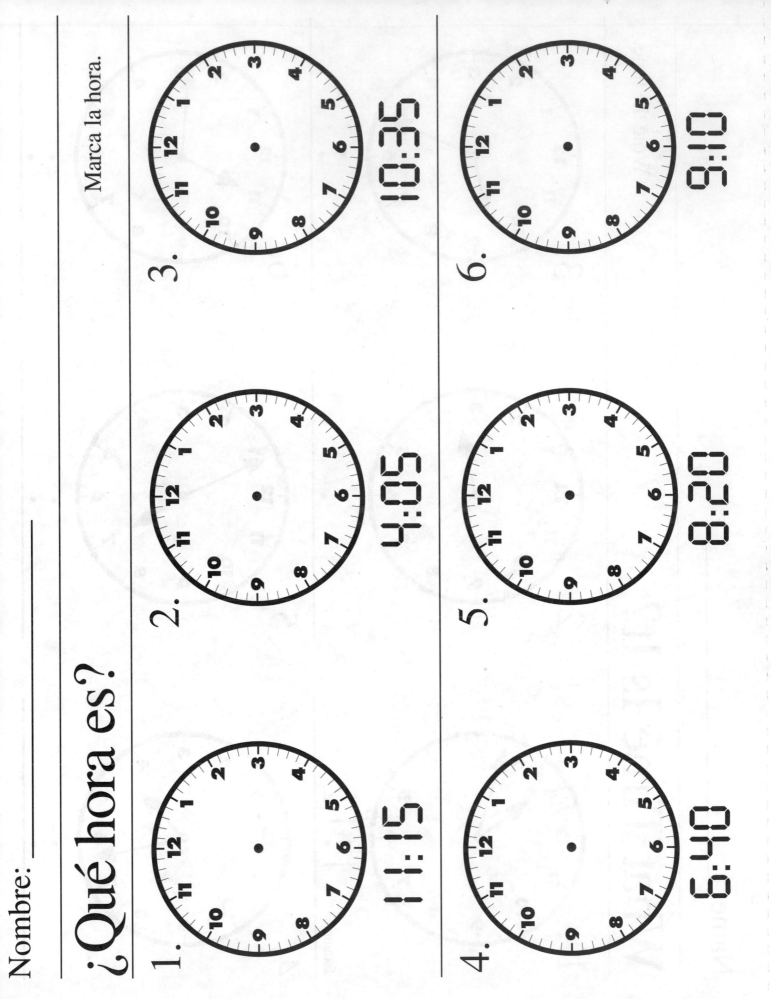

1. 11:15

2. 4:05

3. 10:35

4. 6:40

5. 8:20

6. 9:10

Name: _____

What Time Is It?

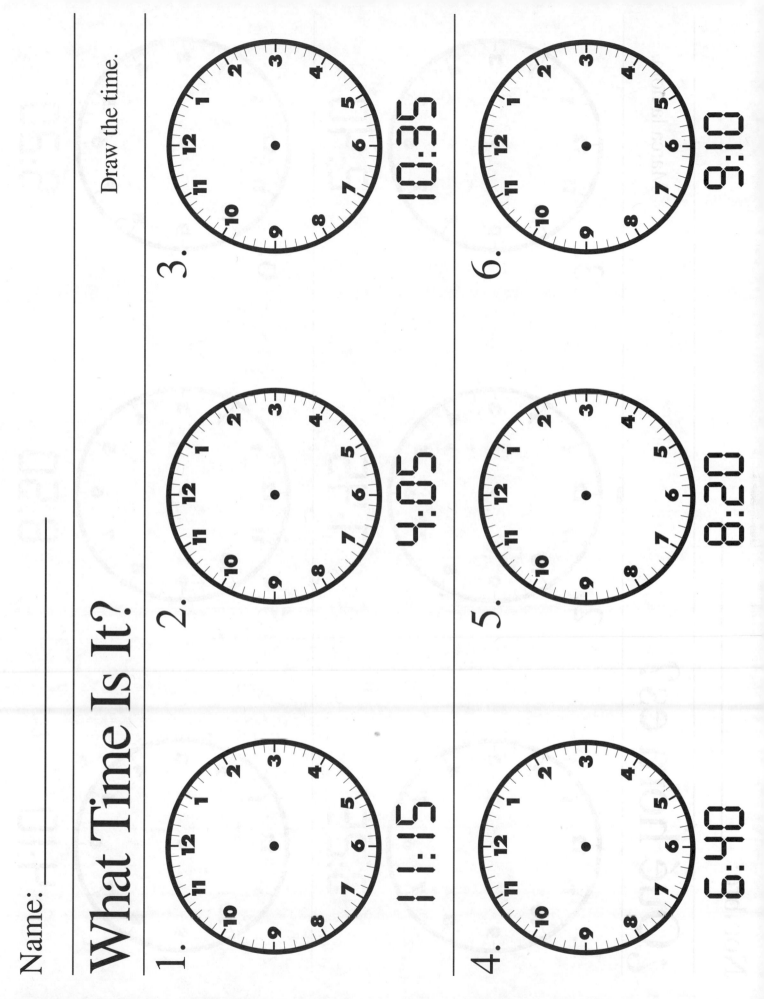

1.   11:15

2.   4:05

3.   10:35

4.   6:40

5.   8:20

6.   9:10

Nombre: _____

¿Qué hora es?

Marca la hora.

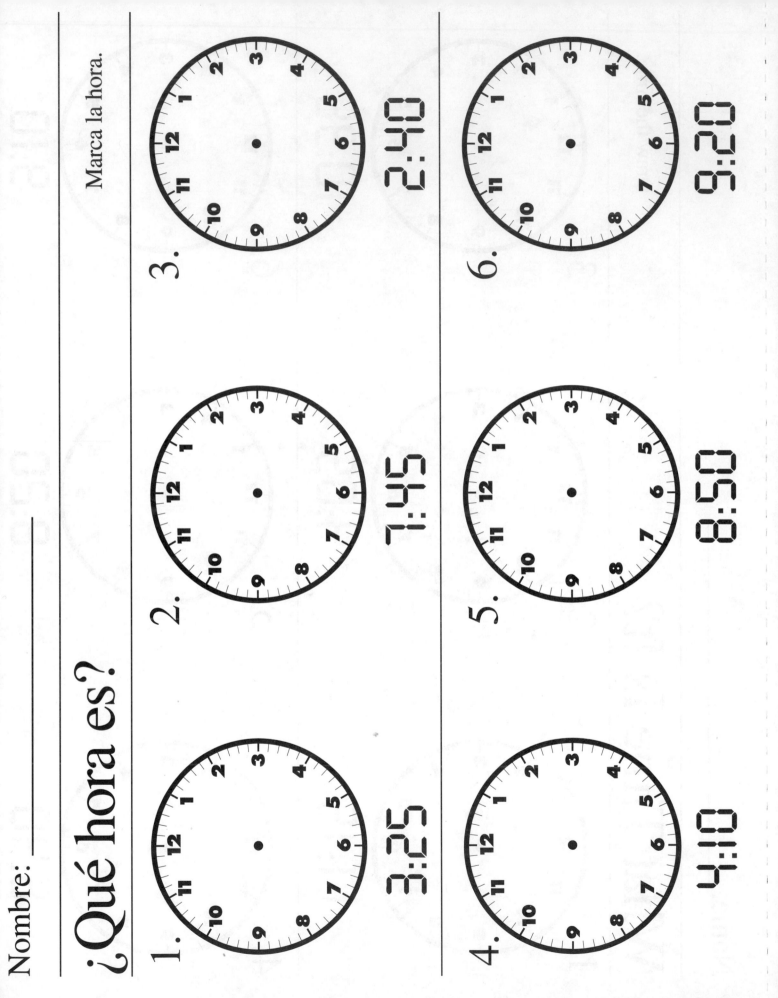

1. 3:25

2. 7:45

3. 2:40

4. 4:10

5. 8:50

6. 9:20

What Time Is It?

Draw the time.

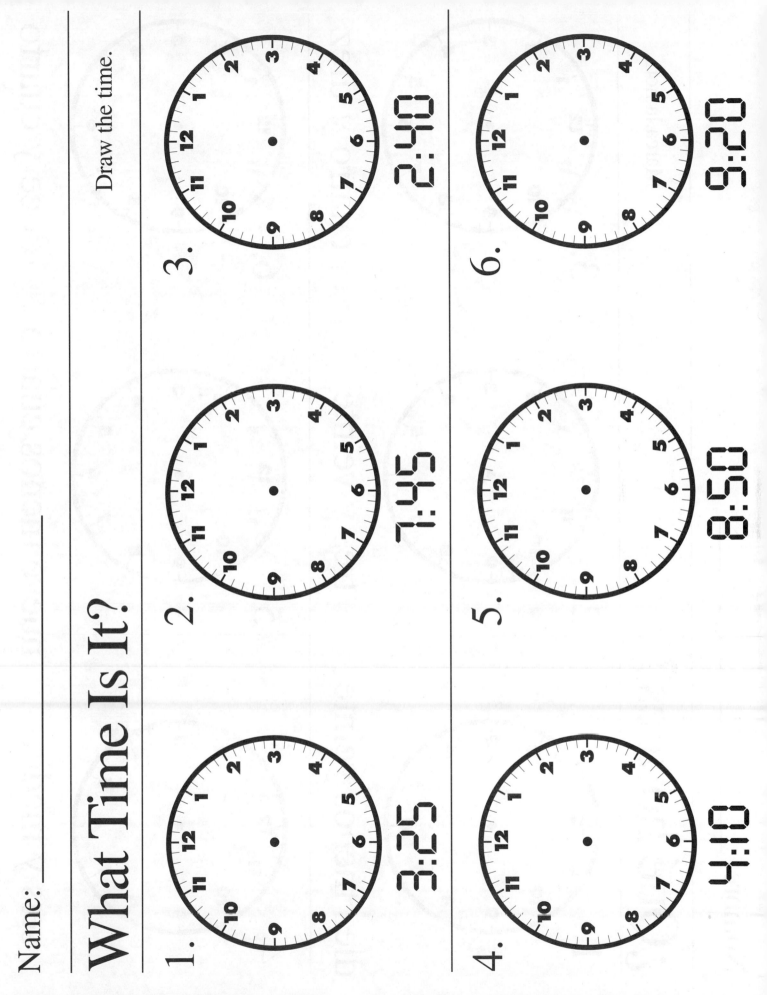

1.

3:25

2.

7:45

3.

2:40

4.

4:10

5.

8:50

6.

9:20

Nombre: _____

¿Qué hora es?

Marca la hora.

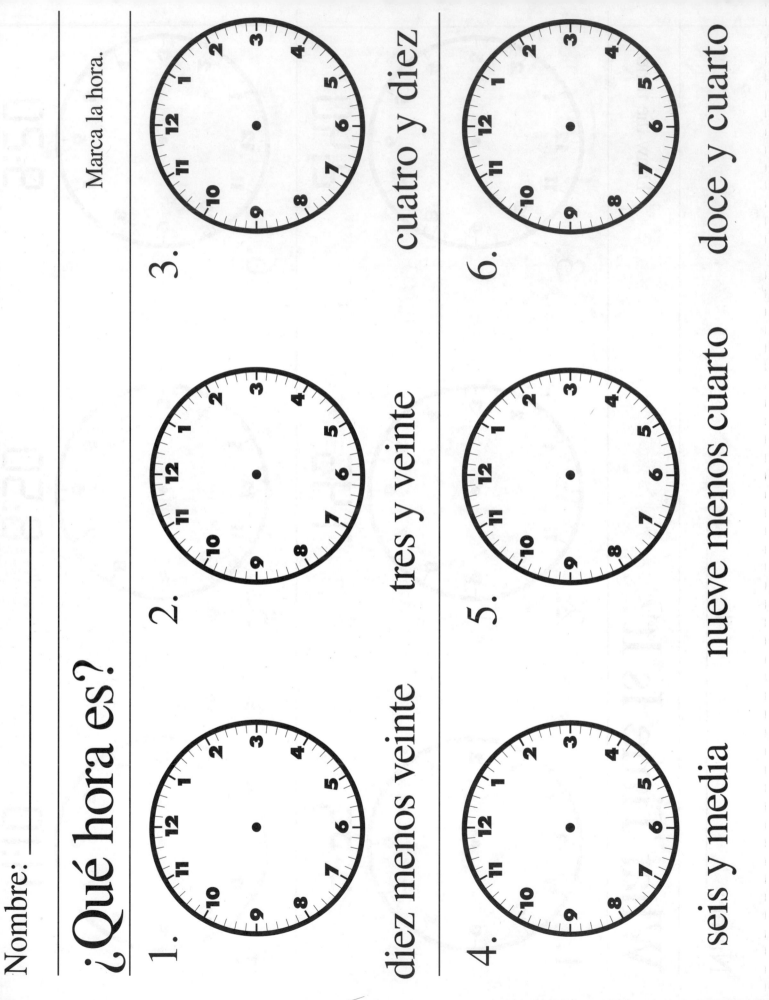

1.

2.

tres y veinte

3.

cuatro y diez

diez menos veinte

4.

seis y media

5.

nueve menos cuarto

6.

doce y cuarto

Name: _____

What Time Is It?

Draw the time.

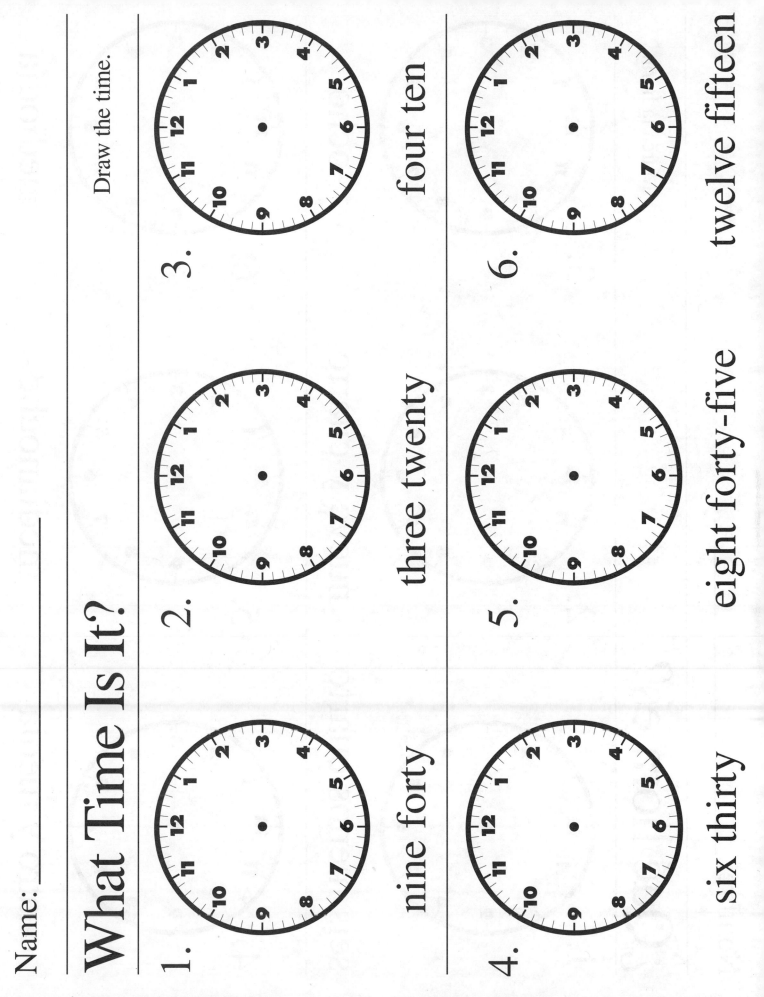

1.

2. three twenty

3. four ten

4. six thirty

5. eight forty-five

6. twelve fifteen

nine forty

Nombre: _____

¿Qué hora es?

Marca la hora.

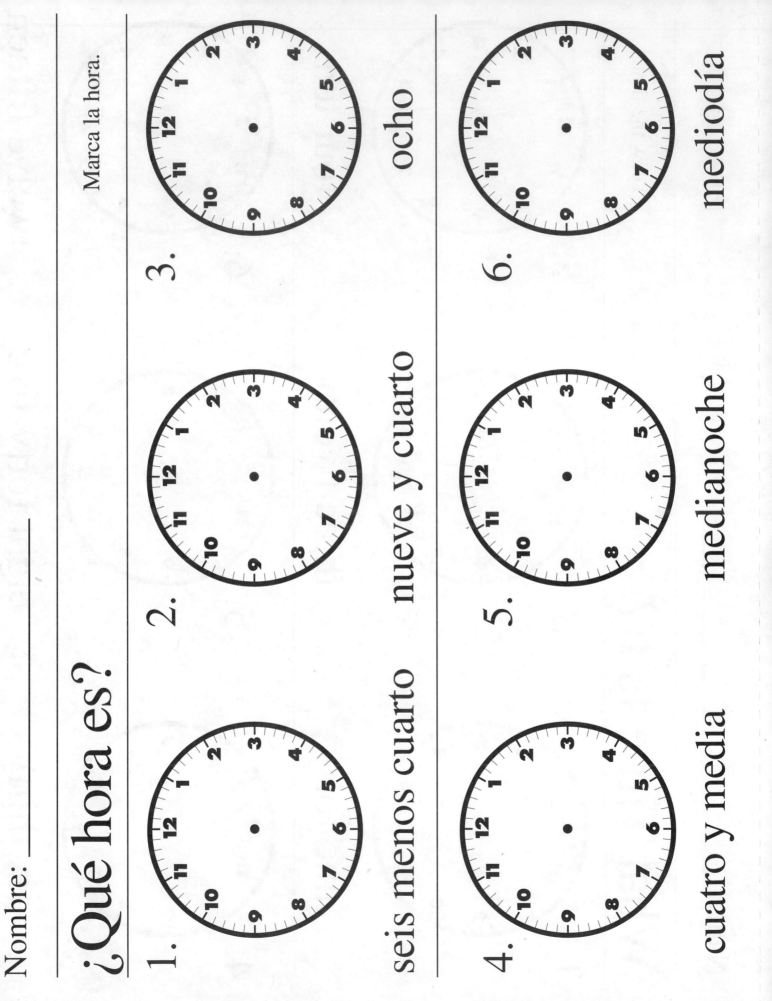

1.

2. nueve y cuarto

3. ocho

seis menos cuarto

4. cuatro y media

5. medianoche

6. mediodía

Name: _____

What Time Is It?

Draw the time.

1.

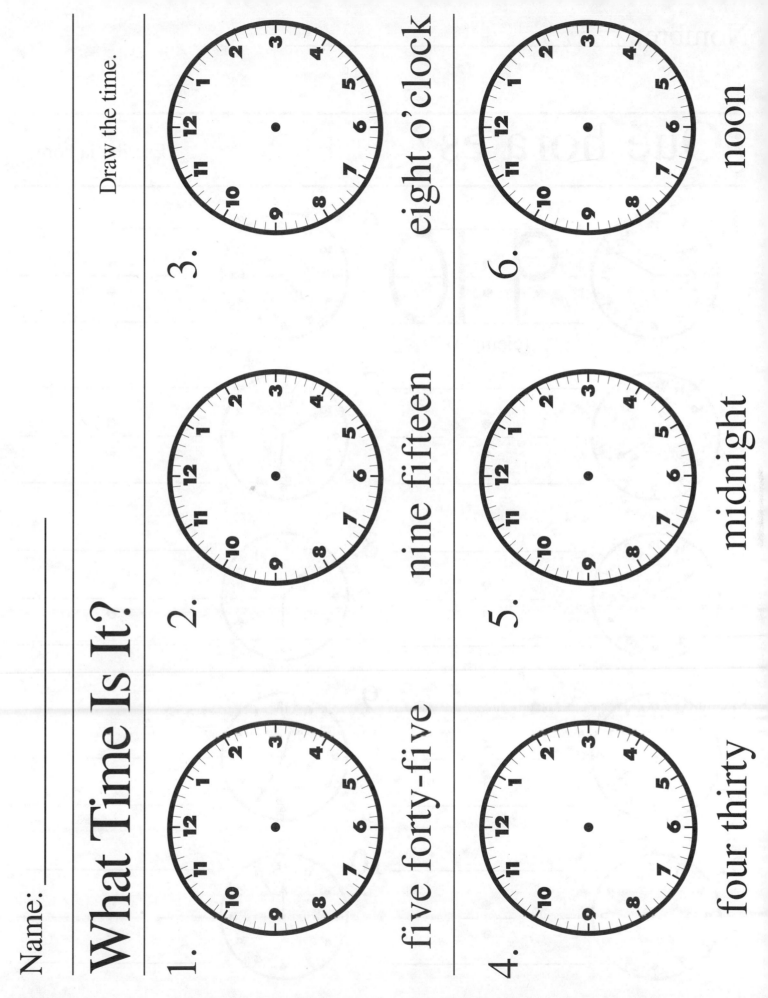

five forty-five

2.

nine fifteen

3.

eight o'clock

4.

four thirty

5.

midnight

6.

noon

¿Qué hora es?

Escribe la hora.

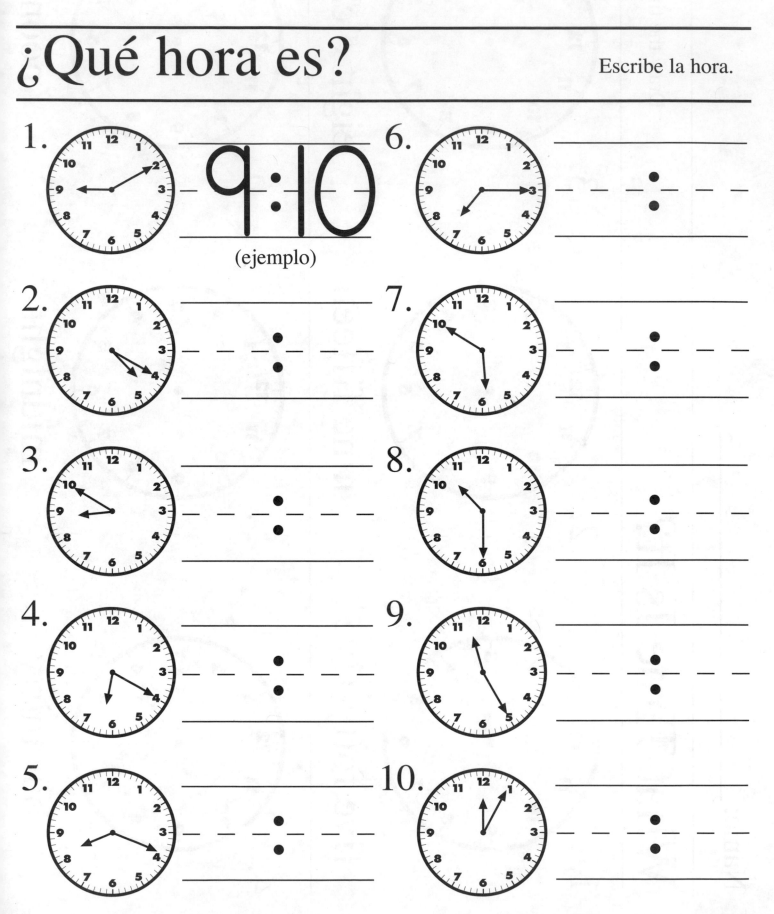

1. **9:10**

(ejemplo)

2. ___:___

3. ___:___

4. ___:___

5. ___:___

6. ___:___

7. ___:___

8. ___:___

9. ___:___

10. ___:___

Name:_____

What Time Is It?

Write the time.

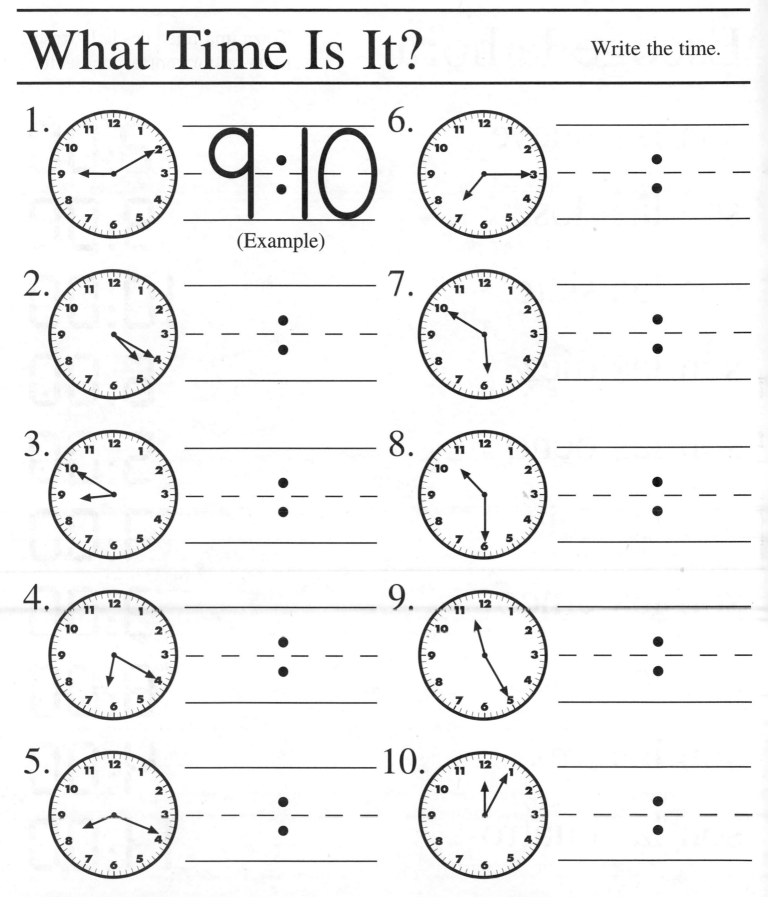

1. 9:10 (Example)

2.

3.

4.

5.

6.

7.

8.

9.

10.

Escoge la hora

Traza una línea desde la frase hasta la hora correspondiente.

son las nueve	2:00
son las dos	9:00
son las siete	10:00
son las diez	6:00
son las ocho	5:00
son las seis	7:00
son las cinco	3:00
son las once	8:00
son las tres	4:00
son las cuatro	11:00

Time Match

Draw a line to the correct time.

nine o'clock	2:00
two o'clock	9:00
seven o'clock	10:00
ten o'clock	6:00
eight o'clock	5:00
six o'clock	7:00
five o'clock	3:00
eleven o'clock	8:00
three o'clock	4:00
four o'clock	11:00

Escoge la hora

Traza una línea desde la frase hasta la hora correspondiente.

son las nueve y media   10:30

son las dos y media   9:30

son las siete y media   2:30

son las diez y media   7:30

son las ocho y media   6:30

son las seis y media   8:30

son las cinco y media   3:30

son las once y media   5:30

son las tres y media   4:30

son las cuatro y media   11:30

Time Match
Draw a line to the correct time.

nine thirty	10:30
two thirty	9:30
seven thirty	2:30
ten thirty	7:30
eight thirty	6:30
six thirty	8:30
five thirty	3:30
eleven thirty	5:30
three thirty	4:30
four thirty	11:30

Busca las palabras

¿Puedes encontrar las palabras escondidas?
Hicimos un círculo alrededor de "día."
¿Puedes encontrar las demás palabras?

```
m  t  a  i  m  a  ñ  a  n  a
a  u  a  t  i  e  m  p  o  s
d  a  c  n  o  c  h  e  m  m
r  h  s  s  e  l  h  e  e  i
u  e  e  e  e  e  r  g  d  l
g  y  i  g  o  v  n  h  i  r
a  m  i  n  u  t  o  o  o  e
d  e  g  n  a  r  r  t  d  l
a  y  r  d  h  o  r  a  í  o
a  m  b  o  b  d  í  a  a  j
```

día   reloj   tiempo

noche   hora   mediodía

mañana   minuto   madrugada

Word Find

Can you find the hidden words?
One word is circled for you.
Find the other words.

```
e  e  r  l  h  h  l  e  h  o  r  l
l  s  e  m  o  e  w  a  t  c  h  e
e  r  m  o  i  n  n  s  n  v  h  o
f  l  v  r  e  v  t  s  t  r  m  n
d  o  s  n  s  f  r  t  p  s  i  m
d  r  e  i  t  i  m  e  t  i  n  i
e  o  c  n  l  n  h  l  f  f  u  h
e  e  o  g  k  b  o  e  c  p  t  o
m  s  n  i  g  h  t  e  n  o  e  u
c  b  d  m  r  i  t  t  o  n  o  r
t  s  d  a  y  t  c  l  o  c  k  s
t  e  u  t  h  o  h  o  n  t  o  c
```

day	clock	time	hour
night	watch	noon	morning
	second	minute	

Answer Key

Pages 40–41

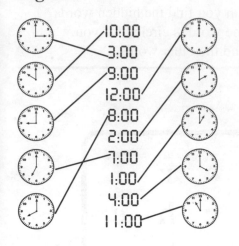

10:00
3:00
9:00
12:00
8:00
2:00
7:00
1:00
4:00
11:00

Page 42

son las dos
son las seis
son las tres
son las cinco
son las cuatro
son las diez
son las doce
son las nueve
es la una
son las siete

Page 43

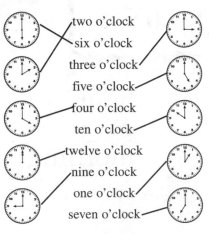

two o'clock
six o'clock
three o'clock
five o'clock
four o'clock
ten o'clock
twelve o'clock
nine o'clock
one o'clock
seven o'clock

Page 44

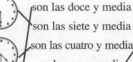

son las doce y media
son las siete y media
son las cuatro y media
es la una y media
son las ocho y media
son las dos y media
son las tres y media
son las cinco y media
son las seis y media
son las diez y media

Page 45

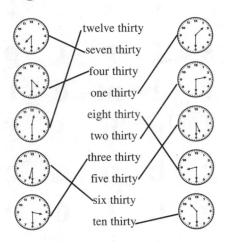

twelve thirty
seven thirty
four thirty
one thirty
eight thirty
two thirty
three thirty
five thirty
six thirty
ten thirty

Page 46

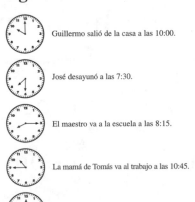

Guillermo salió de la casa a las 10:00.

José desayunó a las 7:30.

El maestro va a la escuela a las 8:15.

La mamá de Tomás va al trabajo a las 10:45.

Comemos el almuerzo al mediodía.

Page 47

Bill left home at 10:00.

Joe ate breakfast at 7:30.

The teacher goes to school at 8:15.

Tom's mother goes to work at 10:45.

We eat lunch at noon.

Page 48

Luis almorzó al mediodía. Tres horas después se comió un bocadillo. ¿A qué hora se comió Luis su bocadillo?

Juan se fue a la escuela a las 8:00. Era una caminata de 10 minutos. ¿A qué hora llegó?

Ana caminó por media hora. Ella empezó a las 7:15. ¿A qué hora terminó?

Lisa jugó con su gato por veinte minutos. Ella terminó a las 9:30. ¿A qué hora empezó?

Tomás se acuesta a las 8:30. Él lee por 30 minutos antes de acostarse. ¿A qué hora empieza a leer?

Page 49

Luis ate lunch at noon. Three hours later, he ate a snack. What time did Luis eat his snack?

Bill left for school at 8:00. It was a 10-minute walk. What time did he get to school?

Ann walked for half an hour. She started at 7:15. What time did she finish?

Lisa played with her cat for 20 minutes. She finished at 9:30. What time did she start?

Tom goes to bed at 8:30. He reads for 30 minutes before bed. What time did he start reading?

Answer Key

Page 50

 Rita cena a las 6:00. Le toma media hora para terminar. ¿A qué hora termina? __6:30__

 David jugó con Marcos por dos horas. Terminaron de jugar a las 3:00. ¿A qué hora empezaron? __1:00__

Ana fue a la tienda a las 2:15. Volvió a casa a las 3:00. ¿Cuánto tiempo estuvo fuera de casa? __45 minutos__

 Susana jugó a "bingo" por una hora y quince minutos. Empezó a las 9:00. ¿A qué hora terminó? __10:15__

 Carlos se va a trabajar a las 7:15. Él trabaja por 8 horas. ¿A qué hora vuelve a casa Carlos? __3:15__

Page 51

 Rita eats dinner at 6:00. It takes her half an hour. What time does she finish? __6:30__

David played with Mark for 2 hours. They finished playing at 3:00. What time did they start? __1:00__

Ann went to the store at 2:15. She came home at 3:00. How long was she gone?
__45 minutes__

Susan played bingo for 1 hour and 15 minutes. She started at 9:00. What time did she finish? __10:15__

Carlos goes to work at 7:15. He works for 8 hours. What time does Carlos go home? __3:15__

Page 52

From left to right then top to bottom: tres, ocho, seis, cuatro, siete, nueve

Page 53

From left to right then top to bottom: three, eight, six, four, seven, nine

Pages 54–55

Students should circle:
1. 9:00, 2. 12:15, 3. 9:30,
4. 6:15, 5. 9:15, 6. 12:45

Pages 56–57

Students should circle:
1. 12:10, 2. 10:50, 3. 11:15,
4. 8:10, 5. 7:20, 6. 3:05

Pages 58–59

1. 12:57
2. 4:33
3. 8:41
4. 10:11
5. 3:19
6. 2:06

Pages 60–61

1. 1:12
2. 3:36
3. 9:26
4. 4:32
5. 7:04
6. 11:14

Pages 62–63

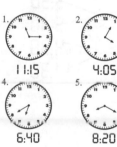

1. 11:15 2. 4:05 3. 10:35
4. 6:40 5. 8:20 6. 9:10

Pages 64–65

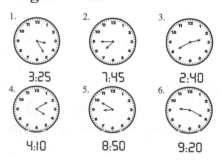

1. 3:25 2. 7:45 3. 2:40
4. 4:10 5. 8:50 6. 9:20

Page 66

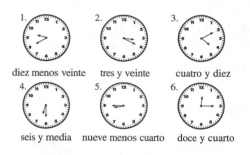

1. diez menos veinte 2. tres y veinte 3. cuatro y diez
4. seis y media 5. nueve menos cuarto 6. doce y cuarto

Page 67

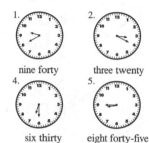

1. nine forty 2. three twenty 3. four ten
4. six thirty 5. eight forty-five 6. twelve fifteen

Page 68

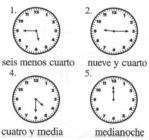

1. seis menos cuarto 2. nueve y cuarto 3. ocho
4. cuatro y media 5. medianoche 6. mediodía

Page 69

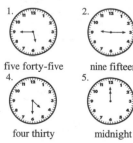

1. five forty-five 2. nine fifteen 3. eight o'clock
4. four thirty 5. midnight 6. noon

Answer Key

Pages 70–71

1. 9:10, 2. 4:20, 3. 8:50,
4. 6:20, 5. 8:19, 6. 7:15,
7. 5:50, 8. 10:30, 9. 11:25,
10. 12:05

Page 72

son las nueve — 2:00
son las dos — 9:00
son las siete — 10:00
son las diez — 6:00
son las ocho — 5:00
son las seis — 7:00
son las cinco — 3:00
son las once — 8:00
son las tres — 4:00
son las cuatro — 11:00

Page 73

nine o'clock — 2:00
two o'clock — 9:00
seven o'clock — 10:00
ten o'clock — 6:00
eight o'clock — 5:00
six o'clock — 7:00
five o'clock — 3:00
eleven o'clock — 8:00
three o'clock — 4:00
four o'clock — 11:00

Page 74

son las nueve y media — 10:30
son las dos y media — 9:30
son las siete y media — 2:30
son las diez y media — 7:30
son las ocho y media — 6:30
son las seis y media — 8:30
son las cinco y media — 3:30
son las once y media — 5:30
son las tres y media — 4:30
son las cuatro y media — 11:30

Page 75

nine thirty — 10:30
two thirty — 9:30
seven thirty — 2:30
ten thirty — 7:30
eight thirty — 6:30
six thirty — 8:30
five thirty — 3:30
eleven thirty — 5:30
three thirty — 4:30
four thirty — 11:30

Page 76

Page 77